Prepare Them to Flourish
By John Whittaker

Copyright 2019 Red Team Ink

Red Team Ink
DBA of Zealot Solutions, Idaho LLC
5447 Kendall St.
Boise, ID 83706
Copyright© 2019 by Red Team Ink

All rights reserved. Without limiting the rights under the copyright reserved above, no part of this publication may be reproduced, stored in, or introduced into a retrieval system, or transmitted in any form or by any means (electronic, mechanical, photocopying, recording, or otherwise) without prior written permission.

This is a work of fiction. Names, characters, businesses, places, events and incidents are either the products of the author's imagination or used in a fictitious manner. Any resemblance to actual persons, living or dead, or actual events is purely coincidental.

For permission requests or information about discounts for special bulk purchases please contact: redteamink@gmail.com. Substantial discounts on bulk orders are available to corporations, professional associations, and small businesses.

Printed in The United States of America

ISBN: 978-1-7322129-4-7

Title: Prepare Them to Flourish
Description: First Edition

John Whittaker

Introduction: Flourish

Flourishing.

That word just feels good to me. It feels vibrant. Alive. Fulfilling design.

I see vibrant mountain meadows, marked by wildflowers and a sparkling stream. I picture lush, green fruit trees, heavy with fruit.

I smile at the thought of a human being fully alive, living the way they were meant to live.

Flourishing. That's the picture Psalm 1 uses for the impact of God's wisdom on a human life.

How blessed is the man who does not walk in the counsel of the wicked,
Nor stand in the path of sinners,
Nor sit in the seat of scoffers!
But his delight is in the law of the Lord,
And in His law he meditates day and night.
He will be like a tree *firmly* planted by streams of water,
Which yields its fruit in its season,
And its leaf does not wither;
And in whatever he does, he prospers. - Psalm 1:1-3

To prosper, in this sense, is not to be wealthy. That's the rather shallow American meaning of the word. The picture here is of a fruit tree whose roots are well-watered, and thus, it flourishes.

Jesus uses similar imagery in John 15.

Here, He compares Himself to a grapevine and his followers to branches. As the branches abide in Him, the vine, His life flows into them and they "bear much fruit" (John 15:5).

It's clear in John 15 that to abide in Jesus is to keep His commands. In other words, it's to live according to His wisdom.

Prepare Them to Flourish

In both Psalm 1 and John 15 the key to flourishing is being rooted or attached to God's wisdom. And that leads to a flourishing life because we are made in God's image, so we're made to function the way God functions.

So what would it look like to raise children according to God's wisdom? What would it look like to raise children who can flourish as human beings?

That's what this book is all about.

To be completely clear from the outset, this book is not a complete guide to what's usually sought in parenting books or parenting classes. In my experience, many people hear "parenting" and they expect to be given a playbook for how to discipline your kids ... and by discipline they usually mean how to correct or manage their behavior.

But there's more to raising flourishing human beings than correcting their behavior!

In fact, correction that's effective is correction that's a part of a much bigger strategy with a much grander goal - the goal of forming wise, good, flourishing men and women.

So instead of giving you a playbook for how to discipline your kids, this book offers you a working framework for how to approach your whole task as parents. What it provides are more like the principles to develop a game plan rather than the exact game plan itself.

And that's far more powerful.

Because, after all, your children are unique. Your circumstances are unique. And let's be honest, by the time your children are 10, 11 or 12 it begins to feel more and more like you're flying by the seat of your pants. The kids are growing up fast. They are changing fast. What's the best thing to do isn't always as clear as it was when they were 2 or 3.

And the best way to fly by the seat of your pants is with a broad, wise, goal-oriented strategy, not a step-by-step plan.

So here's to having a strategy that prepares them to flourish!

Chapter 1 - A Biblical View of Children

I remember the day both my kids were born. My wife remembers all the details of the day ... who said what, what happened when. All of them. It's amazing to me. I don't remember all the details but I do remember how I felt - amazed, proud (of my wife and that I was a dad!), and overjoyed.

My son is my firstborn. And I remember simply feeling awestruck by the thought that I was a dad! A dad! I who grew up without a dad was a dad!

And I was so proud. It was the mid-90's when he was born, and I wanted to find a stage and a crowd and present my son like baby Simba in the Lion King! I wanted to hold him high and show him off and let everyone know this was *my* son!

And when my daughter was born... oh my heart! Right from the beginning she had my heart. Her big blue eyes and beautiful face... I was smitten from the start.

I'm guessing most of you can relate. Psalm 127:3 says, "Behold, children are a gift of the Lord, the fruit of the womb is a reward."

A gift indeed!

And yet it doesn't take long before you realize that they are the most wonderful, amazing, demanding, challenging, exhausting little gift you will ever receive!

I may have thought these things ...

Why are they crying now?!

Will I ever get a full night's sleep again?!

Terrible two's? What about the three's?!

You lost your school book again?! And you coat? Your shoes too? How in the world did you lose your shoes?! Shouldn't they be on your feet?

Why didn't anyone tell me it was going to be like this?!

If we're going to raise these little humans according to God's wisdom, we must recognize two truths about children that stand in tension to each other. I picture these as two poles or pillars and we operate in the tension between them as we chart our parenting course and interact with our children.

* * *

TWO TRUTHS IN TENSION

On the one hand, the Bible attests to the dignity, value, and worth of children. Jesus Himself demonstrates this when He blesses the children. In Mark 10:13-16, some parents bring their children to Jesus to have him bless them. Like security detail for a celebrity, the apostles protest and begin to turn the parents away.

I can imagine them thinking that Jesus was an important Rabbi … He was the Messiah after all, and He had more important business to tend to than blessing their little two-year-olds.

But that's not what Jesus thought.

When Jesus saw what was going on, He called out the apostles and invited the parents to bring their little ones to Him. He said, "Permit the children to come to Me; do not hinder them; for the kingdom of God belongs to such as these" (Mark 10:14).

In word and action, Jesus testifies to the value of little kids. It didn't matter that they weren't contributing members of society yet or that they hadn't made an impact for God's kingdom yet.

They were worth His time.

So, they are worth *our* time. *Our* attention. *Our* energy...just like He gave it to the little ones.

And in addition to being worth our time and attention, according to Jesus there are things about little children that are worth imitating. To ones like them, Jesus says, the kingdom of God belongs. After Jesus welcomes the children and blesses them, He goes on to say that those who enter the kingdom must in some way be like children.

Jesus goes against the grain of His culture (probably most cultures) by placing high value on children.

So we learn that children are valuable and important. They are worth our time and attention. And children have qualities we should learn from and even imitate.

That's the first truth about children.

On the other hand, Proverbs 22:15 declares, "Foolishness is bound up in the heart of a child." In the context of Proverbs, "foolishness" doesn't refer to childishness. Foolishness refers to the inability to make good and wise choices. Fools haven't learned the skill of living.

Characteristics of fools in the book of Proverbs are things such as not fearing God, laziness, having a hot temper, not being able to control your tongue, lacking self-discipline, and an unwillingness to listen to advice. According to the wisdom of the Bible, to be a fool is to go against God and His ways — the very way humans were designed to operate.

So when Proverbs says "foolishness is bound up in the heart of a child" it is saying that all those sorts of tendencies are present in a child's heart. Latent in the child's heart is a tendency towards unwise, immoral self-will.

Prepare Them to Flourish

All parents know this because all parents have experienced it.

A two-year old doesn't need any encouragement to throw a fit.

An 8-year-old can be pretty good at lacking the self-discipline to do his homework.

And just spend time as a "recess monitor" and you'll hear how vicious their little tongues can be.

So we find that children have in their hearts a tendency to go against God's wisdom for their life, and if left to their own devices, life often doesn't turn out well.

So these two key truths stand in tension with each other: children have value, honor, and worth but children also tend towards immoral foolishness. This tension ought to shape everything we do as parents.

* * *

FINDING THEIR OWN WAY ISN'T AN OPTION

One of the main implications of this tension is that we can't let kids go their own way — unless we want them to get lost!

But since they are a gift from the Lord with such value and worth, how could we want that?

So we must help them find their way to a flourishing life. They can't train themselves. If they are going to flourish, they need guidance. They need training. They need direction and correction.

In fact, the full statement of Proverbs 22:15 is, "Foolishness is bound up in the heart of a child; the rod of discipline will remove it far from him." The "rod of discipline" is an image of teaching, training, and correction.

We'll talk more about training and correction in chapter 4. For now, I just want to remind you that God is love and you can't teach God's wisdom in a way contrary to His love. So while the imagery of the "rod" may at first sight sound stern to us, it refers to the necessary task of helping our children learn the wise way to live — not in a harsh or stern way, but lovingly.

Parents must wisely and lovingly teach and train their children, to help steer them away from the foolishness latent in their heart. We need to help them love the wisdom of God, and how to put it into practice in their everyday life. We must help them become diligent and industrious, not giving in to the latent laziness in their heart. We must teach them how to use their tongue in respectful and kind ways. We must teach them that the wise man or woman is the one who seeks counsel and advice and takes feedback, which means we make our home a safe place to do that. We must show them that God's ways are wise ways, that they are the proper soil in which a flourishing life can grow.

We must pray and sweat and plan and labor to overcome the foolishness that is bound up in their heart — and when we fail (which we surely will), we must receive the grace from God to pick ourselves up and struggle once again to show them the way forward.

* * *

INTENTIONALITY REQUIRED

All of this means that you don't *drift* into good parenting. It doesn't happen on accident. Combine the child's latent foolishness with culture's ability to encourage and reinforce that foolishness, and you've got a big job on your hands.

Being intentional is required!

Prepare Them to Flourish

Planning. Praying. Reading. Thinking. Lots of conversations with your spouse. And conversations with people whose parenting you admire (that might even be your own parents!).

One the things my wife and I did that proved to be very helpful for us was writing out our guiding principles and objectives for raising kids. When Louise was pregnant with our son Jeff, we sat down at a restaurant and wrote those guiding principles down. There had already been a good number of conversations during the first few years of marriage about those principles, but getting them down on paper made them more clear and more concrete. I even typed them up afterward and printed them on our old dot-matrix printer (there's a good chance you don't remember those!). Then once a year for the first few years we were parents, we'd pull it out of our files and review the principles and objectives together. Are we on track? Is there anything we want to add, adjust, or change? Are we heading in the right direction?

At the top, we had our big, overarching principle: the purpose of parental discipline is to teach self-discipline. We had objectives about learning the Bible and the value of hard work. We noted how we wanted to be secure enough in ourselves that we could allow our children to be themselves and express themselves. It wasn't a long document... just a little over half a page. But it provided a broad framework of ideas that were important to us as we raised our kids.

It's been 23 years since we wrote those principles down, and we still have that printed piece of paper. I reviewed it the other day with my daughter who was expecting her first child. I hadn't looked at it in over a decade, but what was written there still held true, still made sense, and still would be what I want to aim at as a parent. And I think it served us well as good foundation and framework for our parenting.

You don't have to do that per se. But you do have to be intentional and have a plan. Read good books. Listening to parenting podcasts. Go to parenting workshops. Talk to parents you respect. Have regular conversations with your spouse. Good parenting doesn't just happen on accident. Intentionality is required.

And your kids are too valuable to leave it to chance. They are the most wonderful, amazing, demanding, challenging, exhausting little gift you will ever receive!

Chapter 2 - Goal: Impart Wisdom

I think it happens to most new parents.

You experience the grit and glory of labor and delivery. You've heard the first gasp for air and the first cries of this new little life. You've held her or him in your arms for the first time, gazing at this little person — love-struck. Perhaps you silently hope that their head won't be that shape forever and that they grow into that nose someday (though you wouldn't admit out loud at the time).

And then it hits you.

You're responsible for this little human! They are "yours."

All their basic needs — food, sleep, clothes, love, affection — they are your responsibility!

And what kind of person they become? Well, you will play a huge part in that!

And if you're like me, then there comes that moment of realization — what I have I gotten myself into?!

What am I supposed to do now?

This cute little baby is gonna grow up …

This is a little human being …

He will have his own little personality! She will have he own little will!

How do I raise them?

How *should* I raise them?

And if you're a Christian, there's a good chance you feel an extra burden. What does God want me to do with the little person? It is not just now what or what's the best way to raise him ... but what does God want for this little life? Perhaps it even hits you that there are eternal stakes in this endeavor.

What's the goal of it all? What should we be aiming at?

* * *

THE GOAL IS NOT...

Well-meaning Christians sometimes get the goal wrong. So let's clear some things up right away.

The goal is *not* for our kids to be happy. Obviously happiness is a good thing. God is the most joyful person in the universe. But just making sure our kids are happy is not the goal of parenting. Happiness only comes about from pursuing the true and proper goal of human existence.

The goal is *not* to make sure our kids have good self-esteem. Yes, self-esteem or self-worth is necessary to living well, but once again, self-esteem is a by-product of the proper goal.

The goal is *not* to get your kids "saved." I've known some parents who acted like they needed to make sure their children professed faith in Jesus and got baptized as soon as possible so that they'll go to heaven when they die ... as if that was the main thing they were supposed to do as Christian parents. As important as our kids' relationship with Jesus is, getting them "saved" stops far short of God's vision for your kids.

The goal is *not* for your kids to be good boys and girls. It's not for them to be good Christian kids who behave the way they're supposed to. Again, behavior is important, but if merely making sure our kids do the right thing is our aim we can easily slip into controlling behavior to keep up appearances.

Sometimes this even leads to controlling behavior by appealing to what others think. "We don't do that, Johnny. What would the pastor think? Or what would your Sunday school teacher think?" Or some such thing. This is very damaging. This is a common cause of teens acting one way on Friday night and totally different on Sunday morning.

And that doesn't prepare your son or daughter to flourish.

So what is the goal?

* * *

DISCOVER TRUE TREASURE

In the Bible, the book of Proverbs is a father's advice to his son, preparing him for life. Early on in the book, this is what the father says:

> How blessed is the man who finds wisdom,
> And the man who gains understanding.
> For her profit is better than the profit of silver
> And her gain better than fine gold.
> She is more precious than jewels;
> And nothing you desire compares with her.
> Proverbs 3:13-15

What's better than gold or silver? What's more precious than jewels? In other words, what's true treasure?

Wisdom!

Wisdom is true treasure! How blessed is the man or woman who discovers it!

Over and over Proverbs repeats this refrain. Wisdom is true treasure. Get wisdom!

Wisdom isn't intelligence. Wisdom isn't education or acquiring information. What is wisdom? In the Bible, wisdom refers "the skill of living," the ability to do life well. It is rooted in God and in creation. That is, wisdom is understanding how God created the world and how He designed life to work.

In the biblical worldview there is a way God created things to function. Think of an engineer designing a car. That car is designed to operate a certain and when you operate that way, it works right. You put gas it in not water. You change the oil every 3,000 miles. It's not a bumper car so you don't drive it like one. You drive it, the way it was designed to function.

Biblical wisdom is coming to understand how God designed you and others and the world to operate and learning how to put that into practice in your life. And for us as parents, that also includes passing on to our kids that wisdom about the way life is designed to function.

And that makes life good!

So whereas a fool doesn't fear God, won't take advice and feedback, is lazy, has a hot temper, lacks self-discipline, and other such things, a wise person is industrious and hardworking, controls his temper, doesn't vent, listens to advice, plans ahead, and gives a gentle answer in the face of anger.

One day, your son or your daughter will be living on their own. Will they live wisely? Will he or she live the way their Creator designed them to live and experience the peace and joy that comes from it — what Proverbs calls a garland of grace and a crown of beauty?

Or will they be foolish and bring harm on themselves and others?

Prepare Them to Flourish

You see, *from the moment we bring them home we're preparing them to leave our home.*

And the greatest gift we can give them is God's wisdom so they can do life well.

Wisdom is the greatest possession anyone can have, so acquiring her should be the primary goal of life!! For any of us.

And it should be the treasure we're seeking to pass on to our kids.

* * *

TREASURE CHEST OF WISDOM

Where is this wisdom found? Where should we direct our children in their quest for wisdom?

The answer is found in an easy-to-overlook line in the letter to Colossians. The apostle Paul writes that in Jesus "are hidden all the treasures of wisdom and knowledge" (Colossians 2:3).

Jesus is the treasure chest of wisdom and knowledge!

Getting wisdom = getting Jesus.

So we must constantly direct our kids to Jesus and to the teachings of Jesus. We must immerse them in it. We must help them see how his teaching connects to life in general and to their life in particular. We must help them see that Jesus is the smartest person who ever lived and that He knows how life works best.

If our kids our going to flourish, they must come to have confidence that Jesus really is the way, the truth, and the life! That He lived the most vibrant, flourishing, attractive life possible and He wants to show them how to live that same kind of life.

Thus, we are seeking to impart Christ to them—his wisdom and his skill at living. He is the expert at life. In Him they can be flourishing human beings. This is what the apostle Paul meant when he instructed parents to "bring up [their children] in the admonition and instruction of the Lord." (Ephesians 6:4). We are imparting His wisdom to our kids and we are working and praying for His wisdom to be formed in them.

What does this require of you as a mom or a dad?

Whether it's a million dollars or the wisdom of Jesus, you can't give what you don't have. So to be able to give Jesus and His wisdom to our kids we have to be learning it ourselves. The four Gospels in the New Testament show Jesus in action and pass on His teaching to us. Soak yourself in them. The Letters of the New Testament apply the teachings of Jesus to new situations in life. Read them and reflect on how they intersect with your life.

Learn from Jesus yourself, and then you'll see more clearly how to pass Him on to your children.

From the day they are born, our mission is to prepare our children to live life the way they were designed to live …. with all the skill, all the insight, all the depth, all the richness, all joy, all the fullness that God designed us human being to live with. The ultimate pattern of that and the ultimate source of that is Jesus. Learn from Him. Introduce your kids to Him in the way you live. And help your kids learn from Him and live His way too.

Chapter 3 - Authority - Parents, You're in Charge, but That May Not Mean What You Think it Means

Congratulations!!

You just had a baby!

There's just about nothing more incredible and more amazing than bringing another human being into the world.

There's also no higher calling and no greater responsibility.

You're now a mom. You're now a dad. And whether you like it or not, you're in charge...and you're responsible for this tiny little human - for their welfare, their safety, their needs, their development, and so many other things that affect who this little person becomes.

There's a lot of confusion about what it means to be in charge and how authority is designed to operate. The result of that confusion? Misuse of parental authority, and it's way more common than we'd like to admit.

Some parents are too domineering and too heavy-handed. This type of authority is all about being the boss. It's about making the child do what mom or dad wants or expects. Parents operating from this approach often perceive everything as a challenge to their authority. Everything is a clash of wills, even normal childish mistakes.

Under this misuse of authority, the standards are sometimes excessively high. Occasionally certain expectations are based on the parent's ego - making sure they look good or their child stand out. Sometimes this type of authority is selfish, and attempts to control the child for the parent's convenience. Although this misuse of authority is about being the big boss, in reality this kind of authority is quite weak, and the parent is actually insecure about their authority. This approach demonstrates that the parent doesn't understand what it really means to be in charge and how authority actually works.

Other parents relinquish their responsibility to be in charge. Often, they make the same mistake as those who are domineering. They think being charge means being a big boss ... and they don't want to do that. They don't want to be too heavy-handed, so they make the opposite mistake. They are permissive. Here's a few examples of this might play out:

- You see this when a parent negotiates with a toddler, trying to reason them into the desired behavior.

- A child throws a fit and the parent tries to placate or bribe their way out of the situation.

- Mom asks her kindergartener to do something, and he or she retorts with a loud "No!" A short verbal tussle ensues. The mom sighs in exasperation and just does it herself, just because it's easier.

- A child is throwing a fit or whining or in some way acting up. Instead of actually dealing with the behavior or root issue, the parent hands them a phone to distract them.

- Dad repeatedly asks his 9-year-old to take out the trash or do their homework or perform some other normal task and his child mumbles "Just a minute," and "ok" or some such thing but never budges. The task either never gets done, or dad explodes in frustration at his child.

You get the idea. These parenting actions often derive from giving away parental authority and failing to lead your child.

So here's the thing - mom, dad, you're in charge! You are the authority in your home in relationship to your children. This is assumed and evident in the apostle Paul's instructions to children. "Children, obey your parents in the Lord, for this is right" (Ephesians 6:1). This is the repeated expectation of Scripture: children are to arrange themselves under the authority of their parents. And so, parents, you are in charge.

Now, according to God's wisdom what does that mean? If it doesn't mean being the boss and it doesn't mean being permissive and nice, what does it mean?

Let's begin answering the question by answering another question — why are parents in charge?

* * *

WHAT MAKES YOU IN CHARGE?

Why are you in charge? Is it because you're older? Is it because you're bigger? Stronger? Smarter?

You may be bigger or stronger or smarter for now. But what happens when you're not? I remember when my 14-year-old said, "Well, dad, mom doesn't 'scare' me anymore." What then? Do you cease being in charge? We instinctively know that we still should be, but what makes us in charge? And often it's confusion about this that leads to the battle to maintain control which leads to undue conflict during those teenage years.

Besides, being bigger, stronger, and even smarter don't automatically confer authority on any person, right?

No, there's actually a really important truth about *all* human authority — parents, bosses, presidents, all of them, whether they know it or not.

All human authority is delegated authority. It's not inherent. It's not built-in. We only have authority because it was given to us for a specific role or responsibility.

I think of Jesus' statement before the governor Pilate: you would have no authority if it wasn't *given* to you by God (John 19:11, emphasis added).

The same is true for parents.

You only have authority over your son or daughter because it was given to you by God. *You are in charge because God put you in charge.* And you are accountable to Him for how you use (or misuse) your authority.

This is crucial for you to recognize. It's also important for you children to understand.

"Johnny, do you know why daddy (or mommy) is in charge of you? Because God put me in charge. And just like you have to listen to me for how you act, well I have to listen to God for how I act as a person and as your parent. I don't always get it right, but I'm trying to do what God expects me to and I'll have to answer to Him for that."

We actually something like that to our kids at times.

Now, if you're going to say that, of course you better actually be letting God teach you how to handle the authority He's given you and what it looks like to parent God's way and not your own!

* * *

AUTHORITY THE WAY GOD INTENDS IT

In general, American culture isn't a big fan of authority. We prefer to do it our way, and we say things like "no one can tell me what to do." And even if we don't say that, we bristle at the thought of being "under" someone who's in charge (just check your immediate reaction to that sentence!).

Most likely the reason for this is because we've seen so much misuse of authority that we are suspicious of all authority. To varying degrees, we suspect that those in charge are in it for their own gain, to advance their own agenda and benefit themselves.

How does this cultural vibe affect us as parents? Very often, we struggle to know *how* to be in charge. Some parents as noted above even resist the idea that they are in charge. And oftentimes many of us swing between being too controlling and too permissive. All of which throws our in-charge-ness out of whack.

So how are supposed to be in charge the way God intends?

Let's start by listening to Jesus. Jesus teaches us that authority according to God's design is other-centered not self-centered. To be in charge is for the benefit of those in your charge, not vice versa. This is God's way in Jesus.

Jesus said, "You know that those who are recognized as rulers of the Gentiles lord it over them; and their great men exercise authority over them. But it is not this way among you, but whoever wishes to become great among you shall be your servant; and whoever wishes to be first among you shall be slave of all." (Mark 10:42-44)

What Jesus is saying is, the typical way authority is used by a fallen culture is to be the Big Boss. I'm in charge and everyone needs to know it; and everyone better toe the line! We know Jesus is right because we experience it. Think of the head of your HOA! We experience this at times on the job or in school. Some of us experienced it in our homes growing up.

But in Jesus' kingdom, authority is used differently. Those in charge use their authority for the good of those in their charge. So when followers of Jesus are given authority they don't reject it, as if power and authority are bad things in and of themselves. Rather, they embrace their authority as an opportunity to *care* for and *serve* others.

They exercise their authority for the good of others.

This is costly and demanding, but it is the way of Jesus. "For even the Son of Man did not come to be served, but to serve, and to give His life a ransom for many" (Mark 10:45). Jesus used His authority to lay down His life for others.

In Jesus, we see that God himself uses his divine authority not for His own gain, but for the sake of others. Nowhere is this clearer than in Philippians 2.

In Philippians 2, Paul calls Christians to do nothing from selfish ambition or conceit but humbly consider others more important than yourself (Philippians 2:3-4). Can you imagine how our parenting would change and all our relationships would change for the better, if we just lived out these two Bible verses?!

Paul continues in Philippians 2 by setting forth Jesus as the ultimate example of living this way. He says that Jesus existed in the very "form of God." That is, whatever God is, Jesus was. But — note this—He "did not regard equality with God a thing to be grasped" (2:6). That means He didn't use his position and His authority as God for His own gain or to pursue His own agenda. He didn't cling to His rights as God. Nor did He seek his own well-being. Instead, "he emptied Himself" (2:7). That is, He lowered Himself and poured Himself out for the sake of others. He became a servant.

This is how God in Christ used his position and His power - His authority. This is how God wants us to use ours.

In fact, Jesus lowered Himself so far that it literally cost Him His life — He died on a cross. That was the lowest form of death imaginable in the world of Jesus' day. Crucifixion was reserved for criminals of the worst kind, and from the Jewish standpoint, to be crucified meant you were cursed by God. So, Paul says Jesus went from the highest high — the rights, privileges, and very nature of God—to the lowest low—death on a cross! If Jesus went that low for you and me, can't we also lower ourselves for the good of others, especially our kids?

In fact, this is Jesus' vision for authority. And it's echoed in every passage in the New Testament on authority. People are given authority for the good of those under their authority.

This is how you are to dad. This is how you are to mom.

Parents, you are in charge for the good of your children. Your authority always has their best interest at heart.

Knowing this, we take hold of the reigns of authority in our home, and we humbly, yet confidently, expect our children to respect the authority we've been given. We do this, not because somehow we are bigger and smarter than they are, so they better listen to us. We do this humbly, because God delegated this responsibility to us and He is counting on us to use it wisely for the well-being of our son or daughter.

And by consistent, steadfast self-sacrifice, we demonstrate that they can trust our authority. It is this heart-set, this posture of the soul, that enables us as parents to guard against exasperating and embittering our children. (Eph 6:4; Col 3:21)

We know we're in charge because God put us in charge for the good of our children. Therefore, we don't have to fight to be in charge and we don't have to prove we're in charge. We humbly, yet confidently, conduct ourselves as those who are in charge, ready and willing to lay down our lives for our child and seeking what's best for our child. We may not always get it right, but we can always have that as the aim of our decisions and actions as parents.

And we do this under God, that is, with a conscious awareness that we are accountable to God for the stewardship of our children. Just as our children are under our authority, we are under God's authority, and his assessment of the task He's given us is what really matters. So we humbly, patiently, steadfastly, look to God and depend on Him to carry out this responsibility He has given us.

We do all of this, because under God and in Christ, we know that authority as God intends it is good. It's wise. And it's helpful to the humans entrusted to us as our children.

* * *

YOU ARE RESPONSIBLE

So you have been given authority, and here's what that means. It means you are responsible for what goes on in your home. You set the direction and tone for the culture of your family. You are responsible for the way people talk to each other in your family. You're responsible the way you treat each other and for the way you interact with each other. You are responsible for all of it!

- If yelling is the norm or not.
- If kindness and respect prevail.
- If obedience is expected or not.
- If laughter and conversation are common.
- If prayer is frequent or not.
- What's watched on T.V. and what's not.
- When people are on their phones or not.
- How central Jesus is to life.
- How people respond to each when they fail each other or hurt each other.
- The way brothers and sisters talk to each other and about each other.
- What's a priority and what's not.
- How money is spent and why.

It's all your responsibility. That's what it means to be in charge.

Dad and mom, you are in charge of all such things. You have been given the responsibility for what kind of environment your children will grow up in. You have been entrusted with their well-being.

Will you arrange yourself under Jesus and lay down your life for your family, just like Jesus laid down His life for you?

Chapter 4 - Tools and Practices Part. 1: Relationship, Teaching, and Correction

When you bring a newborn home from the hospital, it's exhausting and a little bit frustrating. But it's not overly complicated. For those first few months they need food, care, and lots of love and affection.

But it won't be long until a good degree of complication gets added to the mix. And it seems like it keeps getting more and more complicated with each new stage. Clarity gives way to uncertainty, and the parenting questions mount.

Here are some questions we ask as parents:

- How do we stop our kids from fighting?
- How do we get our kids to do their homework?
- What do we do when our kids fail to do their chores?
- How do we stop our child from biting (or lying or hitting or ___)?
- How can we get our child to eat their food?
- Our son's room is a disaster, and it smells. What do we do?

All of these are real, pressing questions. And whenever I've led a parenting seminar or course, my experience has been answers to these kinds of questions are what everyone is hoping to get. I understand. In the daily fray that parenting is, these kinds of questions feel the most urgent.

But there are other questions that, in the fog of battle that parenting often feels like, are just as real and in my opinion more important.

- How do we help our kids learn how to be responsible?
- How do we teach our kids to love others?
- How do we teach our kids to cooperate?
- How do we help our kids learn to be respectful?
- How do we train our kids to manage money?
- How do we prepare our children to adult?

And other questions like these.

Notice the first set of questions are reactive. They are looking to correct something that has gone wrong. They focus on fixing something that's broken. The second set of questions, on the other hand, are proactive. They seek to instill habits and skills to help things go right.

Which kind of questions do we find ourselves spending more time on as parents? Which kind of questions would you say are more fundamental for preparing our children to flourish?

Here's the thing: it's so easy to just react to things when they go wrong rather than working ahead of time for things to go right. What if we made the effort to reverse the way we invest our time and energy as parents? What if we sought to invest the larger portion of our time and energy into the second kinds of questions? What if we worked harder at preparing and teaching and structuring things to go right?

The fact is, if we put the majority of our time and energy into working for things to go right, then our correction would actually be far more effective.

It seems like our default is to think of discipline as correction. But if we are going to raise kids according to God's wisdom, we need to recognize that the word "discipline" is more equivalent to training than merely correcting. Discipline includes correction, but it is bigger and greater than that. Correcting is actually a small part of parental discipline.

* * *

CORRECTION DEPENDS ON TEACHING[1]

What does it mean focus your efforts on working for things to go right and how can you do it? I'm glad you asked!

For starters, we must recognize that correction is only as good as the teaching that underlies it.

---

[1] Note: The material about correction, teaching, and relationship is adapted from "The Parenting Pyramid," by the Arbinger Institute, 1998. I would encourage you to find a copy of this online and read it. It's short but so helpful, and there's really nothing else like it.

Suppose for example that little Sally is seven years old. And you, her mom, decide it's time for her to start loading the dishwasher. She's never done it before but you've decided she's capable now. So after dinner is done, you announce, "Sally, you're loading the dishwasher tonight."

And leave little Sally to it.

The next morning you're rushing around to get Sally and her little brother off to school. You open the dishwasher to put the cereal bowls inside. And you can't believe what you see!

You're already a little frazzled trying the get the kids out the door, but the dishes Sally put in the dishwasher are a disaster! And the tone of your voice makes it clear to little Sally that you are none too pleased!

"Sally, look at this! I can't believe this mess. What were you thinking?! When you come home from school …"

But is it really Sally's fault? Is your irritated correction fair? Is it really going to solve the problem? What does Sally need?

Sally needs you to show her how to load the dishwasher. She needs you to do it with her a couple times. Then she can do it on her own and you can give positive feedback. And if there's a way she can do something better, you can show her again. Sally needs you to teach her. And then your correction will be undergirded by that teaching, and it will be more helpful to you and to Sally.

Teaching is prerequisite to correction!

Teaching underlies correction. If your correction is going to be most effective, you must teach before you correct.

Teaching involves showing not just telling. Show them. Model it. Do it with them if need be. When your teenage son or daughter gets a notice that they're overdrawn in their bank account, don't just chew them out or give them more money. Get online. Look at their account with them. Help them to see why they are overdrawn and where their money is going. Teach them how to manage money.

When your kids are younger, role play to have them practice.

When they speak unkindly or disrespectfully to their brother or sister, have them try it again.

And here's a teaching tip that I think is very important: tie your teaching to virtues. Remember your goal is to cultivate the character of Christ and impart His wisdom. So connect the specific tasks, skills, and behaviors you are teaching to the virtues of Christlikeness.

So, for example, when eating out at a restaurant with small kids explain the importance of respect before you go inside.

"At a restaurant there's a lot of other people eating, right? And we want them to have a nice meal as family. Right? So that means out of respect for them we need to make sure we're polite and aren't too loud. Ok?"

Then when you are sitting at your table and little Billy begins to get a little wound up, you can remind him how important it is to respect the other people around him. So their behavior isn't just a matter of not being rude or making a scene. It's about learning to respect others.

Tying teaching to virtues can be done in many areas. Think of virtues like courage, honesty, kindness, responsibility, and hard work. What specific behaviors embody those virtues? When teaching those behaviors (or even correcting the opposite behaviors) tie it to the specific virtue. I believe this is a far clearer and effective way of imparting the wisdom of Christ to your kids.

The main thing to remember here is that teaching is prerequisite to correction. And that means it's bigger than correction and underlies correction. So, be sure to invest in working for things to go right by devoting the energy and time into teaching your kids.

* * *

RELATIONSHIP UNDERLIES TEACHING

Now, just as teaching is prerequisite to correction, relationship is prerequisite to effective teaching.

Why?

Prepare Them to Flourish

Because your relationship with your child gives you the understanding of them you need in order to know how to teach them. Each child is different. The way one learns is different from another. The reasons one might be struggling to do something are likely different from another. So the more you know your child the more effectively you can teach them.

Not only that, but building a solid relationship with your son or daughter cultivates trust so that they are more willing to take your teaching to heart. This becomes especially true and important the older they get.

Your biggest tool here is time. Time spent together. Time taking an interest in what interests them. Enter their world just like Jesus entered ours.

My son is big superhero movie fan. So when the first Captain America movie came out, there I found myself standing in line for a midnight premier on a Thursday night when I had to get up at 5:30 the next morning. Why? Because it was a big deal to Jeff, and he was a big deal to me. By the way, this has now become a tradition. My son is a young adult now, and we just bought tickets to go to the latest Avengers movie premiere together. What a treasure that my adult son would still want to go to movies with me!

Work hard to build the connection.

- Eat together.
- Read together.
- Ask lots of questions.
- Take a genuine interest in what interests them.
- Help coach their sports teams.
- Listen to their stories.
- Go out to lunch.
- Spend time together.
- Discover what they enjoy and find ways to do it with them or be involved in it with them.

All of this will help you build a relationship of influence with your child so that you can more effectively impart the wisdom of Jesus to them.

So both building a relationship with your child and teaching your child ought to get more of your attention and energy than correction if you are going to prepare your children to flourish. Both of them are critical to working for things to go right. Investing yourself in them is what it means to reverse the order and invest the majority of your energy into working for things to go right. And then, when you do have to correct, you can do so with much more understanding of your child and much more credibility.

* * *

ONE-ANOTHER CULTURE

Parenting like this requires us to cultivate what I call a "one-another culture" in our home. And once again, this is God's design. The New Testament is loaded with *one anothers*.

- Love one another. (John 13:34)
- Be of the same mind with one another. (Romans 12:16, 15:5)
- Don't boastfully challenge or envy one another. (Galatians 5:26)
- Gently, patiently put up with one another. (Ephesians 4:2)
- Be kind, tender-hearted, and forgiving to one another. (Eph. 4:32)
- Bear with and forgive one another. (Colossians 3:13)
- Confess sins to one another. (James 5:16)
- Through love, serve one another. (Galatians 5:13)
- Be devoted to one another in love. (Romans 12:10)
- Give preference to one another in honor. (Romans 12:10)
- Regard one another as more important than yourselves. (Philippians 2:3)
- Clothe yourselves with humility toward one another. (1 Peter 5:5)
- Bear one another's burdens. (Galatians 6:2)
- Encourage and build up one another. (1 Thessalonians 5:11)
- Spur one another to love and good deeds. (Hebrews 10:24)
- Pray for one another. (James 5:16)

Prepare Them to Flourish

This is the relational culture God wants for his family, the Church. Certainly as followers of Jesus this is the culture we should be seeking to create in our homes with our family. Study this list. Reflect on it. Imagine what it would look like for these *one anothers* to be routinely and consistently lived out in your home. Think about how to encourage your kids to practice them — but remember these kinds of things are better caught than taught. So, dad and mom, you practice these things. You actively love one another. You talk to each other and to your kids in ways that build them up. You lay down your life for each other and serve each other. Then the environment of your home will be like this.

As you do so, you will create a culture in which relationship building and teaching can receive the attention and energy they deserve.

And you'll create a greenhouse in which your kids can be prepared to flourish.

Chapter 5-Tools and Practices Part 2: Aim for Influence

Parenting is discipleship.

As your child grows, you are working for him or her to become mature in Christ. That's what it means to be a mature human being. The more Christ-like you are, the more human you are. So that's what it takes to flourish. That's why parenting is discipleship — we are helping them learn how to live the way they were designed to live from Jesus, the expert at life.

So from day one, we are aiming in this direction through every stage of their development.

By the time your child is ready to leave home, your parental discipline must give way to self-discipline. That's been the goal all along — to prepare them to flourish on their own.

So as your child grows, you need to make sure you don't try to control all of their behavior. That will stunt their growth and hinder them from developing the self-control they will need to flourish on their own.

So in their early years, your children should learn that they can **trust** you. That you will be there for them. That their needs—physical, emotional, and spiritual will be met to the best of your ability. They need to experience that your position of authority as their dad or mom will be used for their good and not in self-seeking or self-serving ways.

They need to experience this **self-giving, loving use of authority** as you begin to teach and correct their behavior. When they begin to assert their own will, they need to experience firm but gentle and kind training to submit to your authority.

As they continue to grow, you should help them pay attention to their **attitudes** and **motivations** underlying their behavior or expressed in their words. You'll also need allow them the space to make mistakes and experience the **consequences** of their choices (e.g., going to school without a jacket because they misplaced it, getting a 0 on assignments because they didn't get them done, not going to a movie with friends because they spent their money on something else, etc.). You'll have to use love and wisdom to discern the best way to do this, and then thoughtfully work through those consequences together with them.

As your son or daughter enters high school, the major objective is to make sure they can take **responsibility** for their actions and are demonstrating growing **wisdom** for life.

That means, you must begin handing over more and more control of their life to them. You need to give the freedom to make their own decisions, all the while knowing they are going to make some bad ones. You also need to stay relationally connected so that you can be a person of influence in their life. Keep the long-range vision in mind. They may not always want your influence at first, but someday...

All of this assumes the interplay of control and influence throughout the parenting experience.

* * *

WORKING TOWARDS INFLUENCE[2]

In order to prepare our kids to flourish, we need to parent in sync with the control-influence dynamic over the course of your child's life. Take a look at the chart above that shows the relationship between control and

---

[2] This section is adapted from *Shepherding a Child's Heart*, by Tedd Tripp. 1995.

influence over the course of your child's growing up years. The blue line represents control. The orange line represents influence.

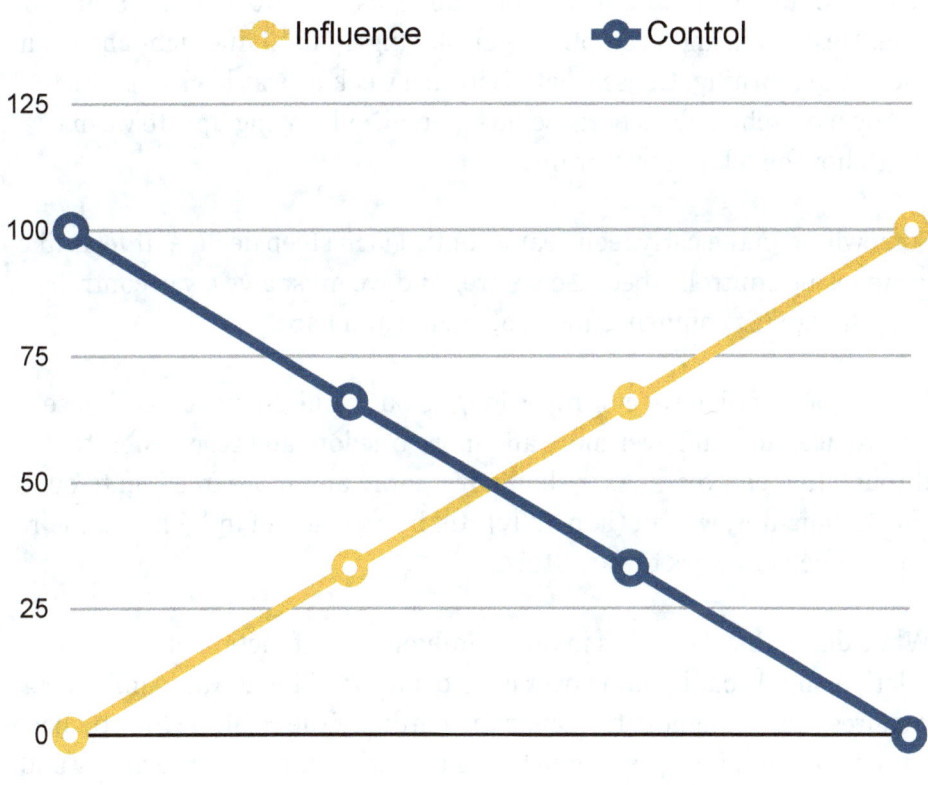

When you bring a brand new baby home, you have 100 percent control over what goes on in your child's life. What they eat. What they wear. Everything. Over the next 18 years that control continually decreases. This happens whether you want it to or not, whether you grind your gears against it or not. So you would be wise to acknowledge that this is going to happen and intentionally hand over control in wise and appropriate ways which help prepare your child to flourish.

Prepare Them to Flourish

I remember the time my 13-year-old told me that all of his friends could stay up as late as they wanted and it wasn't fair that he couldn't do that. He insisted he should be able to go to bed whenever he wanted. So we discussed it and said that was fine, as long as no matter how tired he was he still got up by 6:30 in the morning and was ready to leave for school on time. He agreed, and promptly began staying up until midnight and even one in the morning. Guess what? Within a week he was back to going to bed by 9 on school days because he had realized staying up late wasn't worth how he felt in the morning!

Somewhere in the early teen years, control is in steep decline. It feels like we're losing control … because we are. And we must give away control, even though it's confusing and challenging and hard.

We obviously still have control as long as our children live in our house, but we need to hand over more and more freedom and responsibility through the teen years. As we hand over more and more freedom to our son or daughter, we can (hopefully) still be a person of influence in their life. We need to work towards this.

While doing this, keep this in mind: influence is a function of relationship. What handing over control and working towards influence requires is a willingness to change the nature of the relationship you have with your child. Like pretty much all transitions, this is a little messy and confusing. There will be bumps in the road and mistakes along the way. But in order to work with where your relationship with your child is heading — adulthood and independence — we must do our best to navigate this transition and adjust our relationship with them.

This means, we should be moving more and more into the role of a guide. Instead of always telling, we practice asking. We ask questions to help them see. We debrief and process what's going on within them, to help them understand themselves more. When they make mistakes, we help them figure out why. We're more of a mentor and coach.

This requires us to keep the lines of communication open. We must find ways to connect and spend time with them. One friend of mine used to go get coffee with his teenaged daughter regularly, even though a lot of the time she hardly said a word. He continued to do sit through silent coffee get-togethers, he said, because it provided the opportunity to talk when she felt like talking. We need to be available to talk when they want to talk, which is often at inconvenient times. And talking with them often means listening more than speaking ... which, frankly, is challenging when what they're saying is off base and you know it, but it's not worth arguing about.

It's less important to be right and win an argument than it is to stay connected. So choose your battles wisely. There are still times where you'll need to draw a firm line. Draw it, but don't argue about it. You won't win, because silently in their mind your teenager will still deem you wrong and themselves right. Don't sweat it. Winning the argument isn't that important. Their well-being is. And the only reason you should draw the firm line in the first place is that you're convinced you're drawing it for their well-being.

This process is hard. It's not clear when to give away control and how much to hand over. And your teenager is going to make demands and assertions that aren't always accurate, wise, or fair. At times, their words or actions will sting. And you're going to experience a lot of uncertainty - control is clearer and easier.
Not only that, you and your spouse may not always be on the same page as you're handing over control. You may experience more conflict because of that. This whole process is demanding. Tiring. Confusing. Frustrating.

And it's all that for everybody, you and your child. And bear in mind all the physical and social and emotional changes that your son or daughter is experiencing. Grace, much grace, is the order of the day.

* * *

CLIMATE OF COMMUNICATION

In order to do this well, the key practice is creating a *climate of communication* in your home beginning from day one. In fact, so many of the *one anothers* mentioned at the end of the last chapter deal with the way we talk to each other. And hopefully you heard how vital this is in the paragraphs above. If we're going to teach, train, and coach our children to grow into adults who flourish, it's going to take all kinds of communication … and this needs to be a part of the culture in our home right from the beginning.

- Encouragement
- Challenge
- Warning
- Compliments
- Affirmation
- Affectionate words
- Explaining
- Apologizing
- Teaching
- Questions
- Playful words that bring laughter.
- Small talk about your day.

Not only that, *listening* is going to be key, especially as our children grow older. We need to hear what they are saying. We need to listen closely enough to hear what lies behind the words. We need to take the time to understand them before we try to make them understand us.

You need to engage. Put down the phone. Quit scrolling through social media. Turn off the T.V. Pay attention. Eat dinner together around the table and talk about your days. Tell stories and laugh. Discuss struggles. Teach your kids how to express their feelings well, with accuracy, honesty, and respect. Create a climate of communication. This is crucial to parenting according to God's wisdom, and is key to becoming a person of influence in your son or daughter's life.

Conclusion: Grace

Parenting is a high calling and a noble endeavor. It's not for the faint of heart.

And you will fail.

How do I know? Because I've been there and done that ... and failed more times that I care to count.

But even failure can lead to parenting wins, because in God's wisdom and goodness, failure is met with grace!

So when we fail, we get the beautiful opportunity to display the wisdom of God's grace!

As the gospel takes more and more root in our heart, grace moves more to the center of our home. We know that it is only by the grace of God that we are what we are. We know that He is merciful and compassionate, abounding in steadfast love ... for us, for our spouse, and for our kids. We know that He loves us like that not because we always do it right or because we deserve it. We know that He literally loves us to death in the person of Jesus.

And because of that, we can now drink long and deep at the fountain of His gracious love for us that has forgiven all our failures and sins.

Because of this, we know there is grace for our failures and mistakes as parents. Therefore, we can be honest about them — honest with God, honest with ourselves, honest with our spouse, and even honest with our kids when necessary. We don't need to hide them. We don't need to blame others for them. We don't need to minimize or excuse them. We can honestly confess them, and receive fresh grace to move forward.

Prepare Them to Flourish

And because we have come to know the grace of God in Jesus, we can extend grace to our kids. And we can point them to source of grace, God Himself.

Now let's be really clear about how grace works. Grace doesn't sweep our sins and faults under the carpet. Grace doesn't pretend like our failures are no big deal. It doesn't rationalize or minimize or blame or excuse.

Grace names sin for what it is. And then grace cancels our debt, and gladly welcomes us into loving arms.

Naming and forgiving the wrong; welcoming the wrongdoer. That's how grace works.

You see this in the life of Jesus. He never minimizes or excuses sin. But he freely and gladly forgives it, welcoming the person who did wrong into relationship with Himself.

And you see this in His death. He took sin so seriously He died for our sins, so that He could gladly and freely cancel our debt and welcome us to Himself.

May we look on Him so consistently that His grace daily pours into our soul, so that when we look in the mirror and see our shortcomings and failures, both as a parent and in other ways, we can respond with gratitude and not despair. We can honestly acknowledge them to ourselves and to Him, and thank him for His steadfast, forgiving love. And then may we extend that same grace into our families (and beyond!).

When we do that, grace becomes the environment of our home, and there is room to learn and grow and fail and be loved, just like He loves us!

Because gracious love is the soil in which we human beings flourish.

And the ultimate and eternal source of that love is God! In Him is the soil in which our lives and children's lives can flourish!

About the Author

 John Whittaker has been a Bible college professor and pastor for over 30 years. He has taught the Bible all over the Northwest, as well in places like New Zealand, Australia, and Haiti. His passion is to bring the text to life and to connect the text with life. As a Bible teacher, nothing brings him more joy than seeing people learning to walk with God honestly, humbly, and transformationally.

John met his wife Louise in Bible college when they were both still teenagers. They have been married for 30 years and have raised two children, both of whom are married and starting families of their own. John and Louise love spending time with their grandkids!

If you want to know more about John and his Bible teaching ministry, you can visit his website at http://www.johnwhittaker.net.

You can connect with him through the Bible in Life podcast, on his YouTube channel, or on Facebook and Instagram.

www.ingramcontent.com/pod-product-compliance
Lightning Source LLC
Chambersburg PA
CBHW052044070526
44584CB00018B/2604